INSTANT VORTEX AIR FRYER COOKBOOK:

50 Affordable Quick & Easy Air Fryer Recipes, Fry Bake Grill & Roast Most Wanted Family Meals

LILIANA WATSON

Table of Contents

INTRODUCTION 8

CHAPTER 1: BREAKFAST 12

1. EGG CUPS 12

2. BROCCOLI MUFFINS 14

3. ZUCCHINI GRATIN 15

4. BREAKFAST EGG MUFFINS 16

5. CHEESE PIE 17

6. PARMESAN BREAKFAST CASSEROLE 18

7. VEGETABLE QUICHE 19

8. BREAKFAST EGG TOMATO 21

CHAPTER 2: SNACKS 22

9. SIMPLE PEANUT BUTTER-BANANA BREAD 22

10. CHOCOLATE BANANA BREAD 24

11. CAULIFLOWER POPCORNS 26

12. MEDITTERANEANKALE CHIPS 28

13. POTATO FRIES 30

14. ONION RINGS 31

15. CRISPY PICKLE SLICES 33

16. BEEF TAQUITOS 35

17. TOMATO CHEESE SANDWICH 37

18. ROASTED CHICKPEAS 39

19. APPLE PIE ROLLS 41

20. CINNAMON DONUTS 43

CHAPTER 3: LUNCH 46

21. ALMOND FLOUR BATTERED WINGS 46

22. BABY CORN IN CHILI-TURMERIC SPICE 48

23. BAKED CHEESY EGGPLANT WITH MARINARA 49

24. BAKED POLENTA WITH CHILI-CHEESE 51

25. BAKED PORTOBELLO, PASTA 'N CHEESE 52

26. BAKED POTATO TOPPED WITH CREAM CHEESE 'N OLIVES 54

27. BAKED ZUCCHINI RECIPE FROM MEXICO 55

28. BANANA PEPPER STUFFED WITH TOFU 'N SPICES 57

29. BELL PEPPER-CORN WRAPPED IN TORTILLA 58

30. BLACK BEAN BURGER WITH GARLIC-CHIPOTLE 59

31. SPANISH BROWN RICE, SPINACH 'N TOFU FRITTATA 60

32. BRUSSELS SPROUTS WITH BALSAMIC OIL 62

33. BUTTERED CARROT-ZUCCHINI WITH MAYO 63

34. CAULIFLOWER STEAK WITH THICK SAUCE 65

35. CHEDDAR, SQUASH 'N ZUCCHINI CASSEROLE 66

CHAPTER 4: DINNER **68**

36. PESTO TOMATOES 68

37. HERBED POTATOES 70

38. SEASONED POTATOES 72

39. CHEESY SPINACH 73

40. SPICY ZUCCHINI 74

41. SEASONED YELLOW SQUASH 75

42. BUTTERED ASPARAGUS 76

43. BALSAMIC BRUSSELS SPROUTS 77

44. PARMESAN BROCCOLI 78

45. BUTTERED BROCCOLI 79

46. GREEK BUFFALO CAULIFLOWER 80

47. CAULIFLOWER WITH TOFU 82

48. CARROTS WITH GREEN BEANS 84

49.   BELL PEPPERS WITH POTATOES.. 85

50.   MUSHROOMS WITH PEAS.. 87

CONCLUSION **90**

Introduction

A n Air Fryer does no magic! Yes, it does provide you healthy and oil-free crispy food every time, but it is all science and technology. At first, clear your mind about the basic working of an Air Fryer! It does serve you fried crispy food, but it does not actually fry the food, rather it cooks the food through an entirely different heating mechanism. And that's what you will learn most about in this chapter- the working of an Air Fryer! When it comes to cooking quality food, you cannot really take risks; you got to know all about the appliance you are using. It is worth mentioning here that there are a variety of Air fryer models that are now available, and each varies in size and the control settings according to its brand. We shall look into some general guidelines that will help you use all sorts of Air Fryers with complete ease and convenience.

How Does an Air Fryer Work?

Have you seen or used a countertop convection oven? Well, an Air fryer works pretty much the same except that it has a more powerful convection system that blows hot air through the food at a much higher speed. It is designed in such a way that the food can be placed in a closed chamber right under the fan, fixed near the heating element on top. Every Air fryer consists of the following main components, which together make Air Frying pohoossible.

Air Fryer And The Heating System:

An air fryer is basically a closed cylindrical vessel which has a cooking chamber in its bottom portion and a heating element in the topmost portion. Unlike other cooking appliances, the heat is released from the top of food and then circulates in the cooking chamber due to the powerful convection set up by the fan fixed under the heating element of the fryer. The heating element and fan work together to give your fried food. Besides this heating element, there is also a connected thermostat inside the machine, which regulates the temperature inside the cooking chamber when the heat is produced. The heating element works in cycles to maintain the temperature inside.

Air Fryer Basket And The Fryer Drawer:

The cooking chamber in the Air Fryer is just an empty space, in which a removable drawer is a place. This drawer is used to add food to the air fryer while handling it with ease. This drawer has a handle on the outside and pull-out button on top of the handle to press and pull, otherwise, it keeps locked and fixed in the Air fryer. The food is not directly placed in the drawer; rather, an air fryer basket is placed in the drawer in which the food is place. The basket has a porous base which allows the hot air to pass through the food easily. The basket is removable and washable as well.

You can also use and place other cooking accessories in this basket, like:

- Baking pan

- Casserole dish

- Ramekins

- Air fryer rack

Control Panel and Control Dials:

There is a control panel that is present on the front top portion of an Air fryer. This control panel is usually designed to allow better control over time and temperature settings of the machine. There are two control dials present on the panel:

The Temperature Dial:

The temperature dial can be used to increase or decrease the temperature values on the control panel display. You can select any value from 175 F to 400 F.

The Timer Dial:

The timer dial is used to increase or decrease the cooking time according to the need. Usually, there is a 60-minutes timer dial fixed on any Air fryer.

Then there is a control panel display, which shows indicate the cooking operations. It has different lights to represent a different function. For instance, there are usually:

Red Light: To indicate that the machine is working.

Blue Light: To indicate that the heating or cooking function is over.

Note: These are commonly found features in almost all the Air fryers. There are a number of other side or optional features that are available in different and new models of Air fryers, which are not conversed here.

What Kind of Meals Can You Prepare?

Air Fryers were first launched to provide oil-free crispy food to people looking for low-fat meals. But as the air fryers came more widely in use, new and better uses of the Air fryers came to light. As of today, there are a variety of options on the menu that you can cook in your Air fryer that may include: All Crispy Snacks: Rolls, fries, fat bombs, crisps, etc.

Breakfast Meals: frittata, bread, omelet, bacon, sausages, etc.

Seafood and Fish: Coated crispy cod, salmon, shrimp, etc.

Poultry and Meat: steaks, chops, drumettes, chicken wings, etc.

Vegetables Sides and Mains: Crispy broccoli, Brussels sprouts, cauliflower florets, potato cups, zucchini boat, etc.

Desserts and Fruits: muffins, soufflé, fried fruits, cookies, biscuits, etc.

Air May be Safer than Fryer

Regular frying is all about soaking food in hot oil and leave it there until it completely cooked, browned and crispy. In this process, you need to go extra miles to get rid of all the excess oil, and still, some oil is always left in the food after frying. Due to this reason, the food cooked through regular frying usually has higher fat content, which is not always healthy, especially for those who are suffering from high cholesterol or cardiac problems. Besides, it is not easy to deal with oil frying. Hot oil can be dangerous, and it does not leave the environment clean.

Air Frying, on the other hand, does not use oil as the medium of cooking. The food is not completely dipped or soaked in the oil; rather, it is kept in a sealed chamber where hot air is passed with pressure. The high temperature and high pressure of the air create a cumulative effect that fries the food from the outside, leaving it crispy and crunchy, whereas the overall temperature within the vessel cooks the food from the inside. In this way, the Air Fry cooks food with minimum oil or fat content. Air Frying is also environment friendly as it keeps the surroundings grease-free; all the cooking is carried inside the closed vessel.

Eating Healthy in a World Full of Temptation

Living in the age of fast food and the processed meal is not easy! Even when you want to eat healthily, every other minute, there is a food commercial on your television, tempting you to eat unhealthy food. The whole purpose of using an Air fryer is to control your calorie intake and minimize the fat content to keep yourself healthy. So, it is important to keep yourself away from other food temptations as well and start eating healthy. You can fight your cravings by:

Drinking more water every now and then, and by keeping yourself hydrated.

Consume more protein in your diet through meat and dairy products.

Keep the sugary and unhealthy desserts and snacks away, out of your sight, to avoid cravings.

Meal planning is one good strategy to keep your food free from unhealthy items. Plan your meals beforehand, and cook accordingly.

Continue eating small meals frequently throughout the day to avoid extreme hunger; it will prevent you from binge eating anything.

Stress and anxiety may lead to unhealthy eating practices, so relax.

By getting good sleep and meal at the proper times, you can also maintain good health.

Avoid grocery shopping on an empty stomach; else, you will bring a lot of unwanted and unhealthy food products home.

Practice mindful eating and make yourself aware of your own caloric and nutritional needs then eat accordingly.

Step-by-Step Air Frying

Ok, now that you have unboxed your Air Fryer and it is sitting there on your countertop, you must be wondering what to do next with this thing. So, here are some simple rules to use this machine and to Air Fry food like a pro!

Remove all the packaging material from the appliance. Pull out the Air fryer basket drawer by pressing its pull-out button.

Wash and clean this Air Fryer basket with soap water and then allow it to dry. Place it back into its place.

The basic step is to plug in the device and check it if it is working properly. Its lights and display will automatically light up.

Usually, the Air Fryers are preheated to cook food directly at the desired temperatures. But that's not the case with every recipe.

To preheat your Air Fryer, you must select the desired temperature; first, it can be any value from 175 F to 400 F. Use the Temperature Control Dial to increase or decrease the value of the temperature.

For preheating, it is not necessary to select any time duration. The machine preheats itself according to its own clock.

And once the appliance is heated, the HEAT ON-Blue light will be automatically turned off.

The HEAT ON light indicates the Heating element cycle, which starts and stops in order to maintain the selected cooking temperatures.

When the Air fryer is preheated, hold the handle of the Air Fryer basket, pull it out, and add food according to the recipe, only add food up to 2/3rd full of the basket.

Hold the basket with the same handle and place it back into the space inside the Air fryer.

It is important to slide the Air Fryer Basket Lock to keep the basket in place and to avoid accidental sliding of the basket during the cooking.

Use the timer dial to select the cooking time. The Red light indicates the POWER, and it only illuminates when the Air Fryer is powdered on. It basically shows that the food is cooking, and the timer is ticking.

For instance, if you pull the basket out of the fryer, the RED light will be switched OFF for a while, and the timer will stop. The timer will only resume ticking when the basket is placed back into its position.

When the timer reaches 00 minutes, the air fryer will beep to indicate the completion of the cooking process. At this point, both the Blue and Red lights are TURNED off. Once the cooking session is complete, turn off both the temperature and time dial and unplug the device. Allow it to cool then clean.

Not that you know the glimpse of the Voretx Air Fryer, you can start cooking now by following delicious recipes.

CHAPTER 1:

Breakfast

1.   Egg Cups

Basic Recipe

Preparation Time: 10 minutes

Cooking Time: 18 minutes

Servings: 12

INGREDIENTS:

- 12 eggs

- 4 oz. cream cheese

- 12 bacon strips, uncooked

- 1/4 cup buffalo sauce

- 2/3 cup cheddar cheese, shredded

- Pepper

- Salt

DIRECTIONS:

1. In a bowl, whisk together eggs, pepper, and salt.

2. Line each silicone muffin mold with one bacon strip.

3. Pour egg mixture into each muffin mold and place in the air fryer basket. (In batches)

4. Cook at 350 F for 8 minutes.

5. In another bowl, mix together cheddar cheese and cream cheese and microwave for 30 seconds. Add buffalo sauce and stir well.

6. Remove muffin molds from air fryer and add 2 tsp cheese mixture in the center of each egg cup.

7. Return muffin molds to the air fryer and cook for 10 minutes more.

8. Serve and enjoy.

NUTRITION: Calories 225 Fat 19 g Carbohydrates 1 g Sugar 0.4 g Protein 11 g Cholesterol 180 mg

2.   Broccoli Muffins

Intermediate Recipe

Preparation Time: 10 minutes

Cooking Time: 24 minutes

Servings: 6

INGREDIENTS:

- 2 large eggs

- 1 cup broccoli florets, chopped

- 1 cup unsweetened almond milk

- 2 cups almond flour

- 1 teaspoon baking powder

- 2 tablespoon nutritional yeast

- 1/2 teaspoon sea salt

DIRECTIONS:

1. Preheat the air fryer to 325 F.

2. Add all ingredients into the large bowl and mix until well combined.

3. Pour mixture into the silicone muffin molds and place into the air fryer basket.

4. Cook muffins for 20-24 minutes.

5. Serve and enjoy.

NUTRITION: Calories 260 Fat 21.2 g Carbohydrates 11 g Sugar 1.7 g Protein 12 g Cholesterol 62 mg

3.   <u>Zucchini Gratin</u>

Expert Recipe

Preparation Time: 10 minutes

Cooking Time: 24 minutes

Servings: 4

INGREDIENTS:

- 1 large egg, lightly beaten

- 1 1/4 cup unsweetened almond milk

- 3 medium zucchinis, sliced

- 1 tablespoon Dijon mustard

- 1/2 cup nutritional yeast

- 1 teaspoon sea salt

DIRECTIONS:

1. Preheat the air fryer to 370 F.

2. Arrange zucchini slices in the air fryer baking dish.

3. In a saucepan, heat almond milk over low heat and stir in Dijon mustard, nutritional yeast, and sea salt. Add beaten egg and whisk well. Pour sauce over zucchini slices.

4. Place dish in the air fryer and cook for 20-24 minutes.

5. Serve and enjoy.

NUTRITION: Calories 120 Fat 3.4 g Carbohydrates 14 g Sugar 2 g Protein 13 g Cholesterol 47 mg

4.   Breakfast Egg Muffins

Intermediate Recipe Preparation Time: 10 minutes

Cooking Time: 20 minutes   **Servings:** 12

INGREDIENTS:

- 6 eggs
- 1 lb. ground pork sausage
- 3 tablespoon onion, minced
- 1/2 red pepper, diced
- 1 cup egg whites
- 1/2 cup mozzarella cheese
- 1 cup cheddar cheese

DIRECTIONS:

1. Preheat the air fryer to 325 F.
2. Brown sausage over medium-high heat until meat is no pink.
3. Divide red pepper, cheese, cooked sausages, and onion into each silicone muffin mold.
4. In a large bowl, whisk together egg whites, egg, pepper, and salt.
5. Pour egg mixture into each muffin mold and place into the air fryer basket in batches.
6. Cook muffins in the air fryer for 20 minutes.
7. Serve and enjoy.

NUTRITION: Calories 189 Fat 13.6 g Carbohydrates 2 g Sugar 0.7 g Protein 13 g Cholesterol 115 mg

5.   Cheese Pie

Expert Recipe

Preparation Time: 10 minutes

Cooking Time: 16 minutes

Servings: 4

INGREDIENTS:

- 8 eggs

- 1 1/2 cups heavy whipping cream

- 1 lb. cheddar cheese, grated

- Pepper

- Salt

DIRECTIONS:

1. Preheat the air fryer to 325 F.

2. In a bowl, whisk together cheese, eggs, whipping cream, pepper, and salt.

3. Spray air fryer baking dish with cooking spray.

4. Pour egg mixture into the prepared dish and place in the air fryer basket.

5. Cook for 16 minutes or until the egg is set.

6. Serve and enjoy.

NUTRITION: Calories 735 Fat 63 g Carbohydrates 3 g Sugar 1.3 g Protein 40.2g

Cholesterol 505 mg

6. Parmesan Breakfast Casserole

Intermediate Recipe

Preparation Time: 10 minutes

Cooking Time: 20 minutes

Servings: 3

INGREDIENTS:

- 5 eggs

- 2 tbsps. heavy cream

- 3 tbsps. chunky tomato sauce

- 2 tbsps. parmesan cheese, grated

DIRECTIONS:

1. Preheat the air fryer to 325 F.

2. In mixing bowl, combine together cream and eggs.

3. Add cheese and tomato sauce and mix well.

4. Spray air fryer baking dish with cooking spray.

5. Pour mixture into baking dish and place in the air fryer basket.

6. Cook for 20 minutes.

7. Serve and enjoy.

NUTRITION: Calories 185 Fat 14 g Carbohydrates 2 g Sugar 1.2 g Protein 13.6 g Cholesterol 290 mg

7.   <u>Vegetable Quiche</u>

Intermediate Recipe

Preparation Time: 10 minutes

Cooking Time: 24 minutes

Servings: 6

INGREDIENTS:

- 8 eggs

- 1 cup coconut milk

- 1 cup tomatoes, chopped

- 1 cup zucchini, chopped

- 1 tablespoon butter

- 1 onion, chopped

- 1 cup Parmesan cheese, grated

- 1/2 teaspoon pepper

- 1 teaspoon salt

DIRECTIONS:

1. Preheat the air fryer to 370 F. Melt butter in a pan over medium heat then add onion and sauté until onion lightly brown. Add tomatoes and zucchini to the pan and sauté for 4-5 minutes. Transfer cooked vegetables into the air fryer baking dish.

2. Beat eggs with cheese, milk, pepper, and salt in a bowl. Pour egg mixture over vegetables in a baking dish. Place dish in the air fryer and cook for 24 minutes or until eggs are set.

3. Slice and serve.

NUTRITION: Calories 255 Fat 16 g Carbohydrates 8 g Sugar 4.2 g Protein 21 g Cholesterol 257 mg

8.   Breakfast Egg Tomato

Basic Recipe

Preparation Time: 10 minutes

Cooking Time: 24 minutes

Servings: 2

INGREDIENTS:

- 2 eggs
- 2 large fresh tomatoes
- 1 teaspoon fresh parsley
- Pepper
- Salt

DIRECTIONS:

1. Preheat the air fryer to 325 F.

2. Cut off the top of a tomato and spoon out the tomato innards.

3. Break the egg in each tomato and place in air fryer basket and cook for 24 minutes.

4. Season with parsley, pepper, and salt.

5. Serve and enjoy.

NUTRITION: Calories 95 Fat 5 g Carbohydrates 7.5 g Sugar 5.1 g Protein 7 g Cholesterol 164 mg

CHAPTER 2:

Snacks

9.   Simple Peanut Butter-Banana Bread

Basic Recipe

Preparation Time: 15 minutes

Cooking Time: 40 minutes

Servings: 6

INGREDIENTS:

- 1 cup plus 1 tablespoon all-purpose flour

- ¼ teaspoon baking soda

- 1 teaspoon baking powder

- ¼ teaspoon salt

- 1 large egg 1/3 cup granulated sugar

- ¼ cup canola oil

- 2 tablespoons creamy peanut butter

- 2 tablespoons sour cream

- 1 teaspoon vanilla extract

- 2 medium ripe bananas, peeled and mashed

- ¾ cup walnuts, roughly chopped

DIRECTIONS:

1. In a bowl and mix together the flour, baking powder, baking soda, and salt.

2. In another large bowl, add the egg, sugar, oil, peanut butter, sour cream, and vanilla extract and beat until well combined.

3. Add the bananas and beat until well combined.

4. Add the flour mixture and mix until just combined.

5. Gently, fold in the walnuts.

6. Place the mixture into a lightly greased pan.

7. Press "Power Button" of Air Fry Oven and turn the dial to select the "Air Crisp" mode.

8. Press the Time button and again turn the dial to set the cooking time to 40 minutes.

9. Now push the Temp button and rotate the dial to set the temperature at 330 degrees F.

10. Press "Start/Pause" button to start.

11. When the unit beeps to show that it is preheated, open the lid.

12. Arrange the pan in "Air Fry Basket" and insert in the oven.

13. Place the pan onto a wire rack to cool for about 10 minutes.

14. Carefully, invert the bread onto wire rack to cool completely before slicing.

15. Cut the bread into desired-sized slices and serve.

NUTRITION: Calories 384 Total Fat 23 g Saturated Fat 2.6 g Cholesterol 33 mg Sodium 189 mg Total Carbs 39.3 g Fiber 3 g Sugar 16.8 g Protein 8.9 g

10.   Chocolate Banana Bread

Basic Recipe

Preparation Time: 15 minutes

Cooking Time: 20 minutes

Servings: 8

INGREDIENTS:

- 2 cups flour

- ½ teaspoon baking soda

- ½ teaspoon baking powder

- ½ teaspoon salt

- ¾ cup sugar

- 1/3 cup butter, softened

- 3 eggs

- 1 tablespoon vanilla extract

- 1 cup milk

- ½ cup bananas, peeled and mashed

- 1 cup chocolate chips

DIRECTIONS:

1. In a bowl, mix together the flour, baking soda, baking powder, and salt.

2. In another large bowl, add the butter, and sugar and beat until light and fluffy.

3. Add the eggs, and vanilla extract and whisk until well combined.

4. Add the flour mixture and mix until well combined.

5.   Add the milk, and mashed bananas and mix well.

6.   Gently, fold in the chocolate chips.

7.   Place the mixture into a lightly greased loaf pan.

8.   Press "Power Button" of Air Fry Oven and turn the dial to select the "Air Crisp" mode.

9.   Press the Time button and again turn the dial to set the cooking time to 20 minutes.

10. Now push the Temp button and rotate the dial to set the temperature at 360 degrees F.

11. Press "Start/Pause" button to start.

12. When the unit beeps to show that it is preheated, open the lid.

13. Arrange the pan in "Air Fry Basket" and insert in the oven.

14. Place the pan onto a wire rack to cool for about 10 minutes.

15. Carefully, invert the bread onto wire rack to cool completely before slicing.

16. Cut the bread into desired-sized slices and serve.

NUTRITION: Calories 416 Total Fat 16.5 g Saturated Fat 10.2 g Cholesterol 89 mg Sodium 336 mg Total Carbs 59.2 g Fiber 1.8 g Sugar 32.5 g Protein 8.1 g

11.   <u>Cauliflower Popcorns</u>

Basic Recipe

Preparation Time: 15 minutes

Cooking Time: 12 hours

Servings: 4

INGREDIENTS:

- 2 pounds head cauliflower, cut into small florets

- 2 tablespoons hot sauce

- 1 tablespoon fresh lime juice

- 1 tablespoon oil

- 1 tablespoon smoked paprika

- 1 teaspoon ground cumin

DIRECTIONS:

1. In a bowl, add all the ingredients and toss to coat well.

2. Arrange the cauliflower florets onto 2 cooking trays.

3. Arrange the drip pan in the bottom of Instant Vortex Plus Air Fryer Oven cooking chamber.

4. Select "Dehydrate" and then adjust the temperature to 130 degrees F.

5. Set the timer for 12 hours and press the "Start".

6. When the display shows "Add Food" insert 1 tray in the top position and another in the bottom position. When the display shows "Turn Food" do not turn the food but switch the position of cooking trays.

7. When cooking time is complete, remove the trays from Vortex and serve hot.

NUTRITION: Calories 95 Total Fat 4 g Saturated Fat 0.5 g Cholesterol 0 mg Sodium 260 mg Total Carbs 13.4 g Fiber 6.4 g Sugar 5.7 g Protein 4.9 g

12.   <u>MeditteraneanKale Chips</u>

Basic Recipe

Preparation Time: 15 minutes

Cooking Time: 7 minutes

Servings: 4

INGREDIENTS:

- 1 (8-ounce) bunch curly kale, tough ribs removed and torn into 2-inch pieces
- 1 tablespoon olive oil
- 1 teaspoon salt

DIRECTIONS:

1. In a large bowl, add all the ingredients and with your hands, massage the oil and salt into kale completely.
2. Arrange the kale pieces onto 2 cooking trays.
3. Arrange the drip pan in the bottom of Instant Vortex Plus Air Fryer Oven cooking chamber.
4. Select "Air Fry" and then adjust the temperature to 340 degrees F.
5. Set the timer for 7 minutes and press the "Start".
6. When the display shows "Add Food" insert 1 tray in the top position and another in the bottom position.
7. When the display shows "Turn Food" do not turn the food but switch the position of cooking trays.

8. When cooking time is complete, remove the trays from Vortex and transfer the kale chips into a bowl.

9. Serve hot.

NUTRITION: Calories 58 Total Fat 3.5 g Saturated Fat 0.5 g Cholesterol 0 mg Sodium 606 mg Total Carbs 5.9 g Fiber 0.9 g Sugar 0 g Protein 1.7 g

13.   **Potato Fries**

Basic Recipe

Preparation Time: 15 minutes

Cooking Time: 16 minutes

Servings: 2

INGREDIENTS:

- ½ pound potatoes, peeled and cut into ½-inch thick sticks lengthwise
- 1 tablespoon olive oil
- Salt and ground black pepper, as required

DIRECTIONS:

1. In a large bowl, add all the ingredients and toss to coat well.

2. Arrange the potato sticks onto a cooking tray.

3. Arrange the drip pan in the bottom of Instant Vortex Plus Air Fryer Oven cooking chamber.

4. Select "Air Fry" and then adjust the temperature to 400 degrees F.

5. Set the timer for 16 minutes and press the "Start".

6. When the display shows "Add Food" insert the cooking tray in the center position.

7. When the display shows "Turn Food" turn the potato sticks.

8. When cooking time is complete, remove the tray from Vortex and serve warm.

NUTRITION: Calories 138 Total Fat 7.1 g Saturated Fat 1 g Cholesterol 0 mg Sodium 84 mg Total Carbs 17.8 g Fiber 2.7 g Sugar 1.3 g Protein 1.9 g

14.   Onion Rings

Basic Recipe

Preparation Time: 15 minutes

Cooking Time: 8 minutes

Servings: 4

INGREDIENTS:

- 1 large onion, cut into ½-inch thick rings

- 3 tablespoons coconut flour

- Salt, as required

- 2 large eggs

- 2/3 cup pork rinds

- 3 tablespoons blanched almond flour

- ½ teaspoon paprika

- ½ teaspoon garlic powder

DIRECTIONS:

1. In a shallow dish, mix together the coconut flour and salt.

2. In a second shallow dish, add the eggs and beat lightly.

3. In a third shallow dish, mix together the pork rinds, almond flour and spices.

4. Coat the onion rings with flour mixture, then dip into egg whites and finally coat with the pork rind mixture.

5. Arrange the coated onion rings onto 2 lightly greased cooking trays in a single layer.

6. Arrange the drip pan in the bottom of Instant Vortex Plus Air Fryer Oven cooking chamber.

7. Select "Air Fry" and then adjust the temperature to 400 degrees F.

8. Set the timer for 8 minutes and press the "Start".

9. When the display shows "Add Food" insert 1 tray in the top position and another in the bottom position.

10. When the display shows "Turn Food" do not turn the food but switch the position of cooking trays.

11. When cooking time is complete, remove the trays from Vortex and serve hot.

NUTRITION: Calories 180 Total Fat 10.2 g Saturated Fat 3.2 g Cholesterol 111 mg Sodium 323 mg Total Carbs 9 g Fiber 3.7 g Sugar 1.9 g Protein 13.7 g

15. <u>Crispy Pickle Slices</u>

Basic Recipe

Preparation Time: 15 minutes

Cooking Time: 18 minutes

Servings: 8

INGREDIENTS:

- 16 dill pickle slices

- ¼ cup all-purpose flour

- Salt, as required

- 2 small eggs, beaten lightly

- 1 tablespoon dill pickle juice

- ¼ teaspoon garlic powder

- ¼ teaspoon cayenne pepper

- 1 cup panko breadcrumbs

- 1 tablespoon fresh dill, minced

- Cooking spray

DIRECTIONS:

1. Place the pickle slices over paper towels for about 15 minutes or until all the liquid is absorbed.

2. Meanwhile, in a shallow dish, mix together the flour and salt.

3. In another shallow dish, add the eggs, pickle juice, garlic powder and cayenne and beat until well combined.

4. In a third shallow dish, mix together the panko and dill.

5. Coat the pickle slices with flour mixture, then dip into egg mixture and finally coat with the panko mixture.

6. Spray the pickle slices with cooking spray.

7. Arrange the pickle slices onto a cooking tray.

8. Arrange the drip pan in the bottom of Instant Vortex plus Air Fryer Oven cooking chamber.

9. Select "Air Fry" and then adjust the temperature to 400 degrees F.

10. Set the timer for 18 minutes and press the "Start".

11. When the display shows "Add Food" insert the cooking tray in the center position.

12. When the display shows "Turn Food" turn the pickle slices.

13. When cooking time is complete, remove the tray from Vortex and serve warm.

NUTRITION: Calories 80 Total Fat 2 g Saturated Fat 0.7 g Cholesterol 34 mg Sodium 407 mg Total Carbs 6 g Fiber 0.4 g Sugar 0.3 g Protein 2.1 g

16. Beef Taquitos

Intermediate Recipe

Preparation Time: 15 minutes

Cooking Time: 8 minutes

Servings: 6

INGREDIENTS:

- 6 corn tortillas

- 2 cups cooked beef, shredded

- ½ cup onion, chopped

- 1 cup pepper jack cheese, shredded

- Olive oil cooking spray

DIRECTIONS:

1. Arrange the tortillas onto a smooth surface.

2. Place the shredded meat over one corner of each tortilla, followed by onion and cheese.

3. Roll each tortilla to secure the filling and secure with toothpicks.

4. Spray each taquito with cooking spray evenly.

5. Arrange the taquitos onto a cooking tray.

6. Arrange the drip pan in the bottom of Instant Vortex plus Air Fryer Oven cooking chamber.

7. Select "Air Fry" and then adjust the temperature to 400 degrees F.

8. Set the timer for 8 minutes and press the "Start".

9. When the display shows "Add Food" insert the cooking tray in the center position.

10. When the display shows "Turn Food" turn the taquitos.

11. When cooking time is complete, remove the tray from Vortex and serve warm.

NUTRITION: Calories 263 Total Fat 10.7 g Saturated Fat 5.2 g Cholesterol 84 mg Sodium 248 mg Total Carbs 12.3 g Fiber 1.7 g Sugar 0.6 g Protein 28.4 g

17.   Tomato Cheese Sandwich

Basic Recipe

Preparation Time: 10 minutes

Cooking Time: 10 minutes

Servings: 2

INGREDIENTS:

- 3 tablespoons butter, softened

- 4 white bread slices

- 2 cheddar cheese slices

DIRECTIONS:

1. Spread the butter over each bread slice generously.

2. Place 2 bread slices onto a cooking tray, buttered side down

3. Top each buttered bread slice with 1 cheese slice.

4. Cover with the remaining bread slices, buttered side up.

5. Arrange the sandwiches onto a cooking tray.

6. Arrange the drip pan in the bottom of Instant Vortex Plus Air Fryer Oven cooking chamber.

7. Select "Air Fry" and then adjust the temperature to 375 degrees F.

8. Set the timer for 10 minutes and press the "Start".

9. When the display shows "Add Food" insert the cooking tray in the center position.

10. When the display shows "Turn Food" turn the sandwiches.

11. When cooking time is complete, remove the tray from Vortex.

12. Cut each sandwich in half vertically and serve warm.

NUTRITION: Calories 307 Total Fat 27.2 g Saturated Fat 16.4 g Cholesterol 72 mg Sodium 425 mg Total Carbs 9.4 g Fiber 0.4 g Sugar 0.8 g Protein 8.2 g

18. Roasted Chickpeas

Basic Recipe

Preparation Time: 10 minutes

Cooking Time: 17 minutes

Servings: 6

INGREDIENTS:

- 1 (15-ounce) can chickpeas, rinsed, drained and pat dried

- 1 teaspoon olive oil

- 1 tablespoon dry ranch seasoning mix

DIRECTIONS:

1. Place the chickpeas onto a cooking tray and spread in an even layer.

2. Arrange the drip pan in the bottom of Instant Vortex Plus Air Fryer Oven cooking chamber.

3. Insert the cooking tray in the center position.

4. Select "Air Fry" and then adjust the temperature to 390 degrees F.

5. Set the timer for 17 minutes and press the "Start".

6. When the display shows "Turn Food" turn the sandwiches.

7. When the display shows "Add Food" remove the chickpeas.

8. Drizzle the chickpeas with oil and toss to coat well.

9. Return the cooking tray to the cooking chamber.

10. When the display shows "Turn Food" stir the chickpeas.

11. When cooking time is complete, remove the tray from Vortex and transfer the chickpeas into a bowl.

12. Add the ranch seasoning and toss to coat well.

13. Serve cold.

NUTRITION: Calories 268 Total Fat 5.1 g Saturated Fat 0.6 g Cholesterol 0 mg

Sodium 197 mg Total Carbs 43 g Fiber 12.3 g Sugar 7.6 g Protein 13.7 g

19.   Apple Pie Rolls

Basic Recipe

Preparation Time: 20 minutes

Cooking Time: 12 minutes

Servings: 4

INGREDIENTS:

- 1½ cups tart apples, peeled, cored and chopped

- ¼ cup light brown sugar

- 1¼ teaspoons ground cinnamon, divided

- ½ teaspoon corn starch

- 4 egg roll wrappers

- ¼ cup cream cheese, softened

- Olive oil cooking spray

- 1 tablespoon sugar

DIRECTIONS:

1. In a small bowl, mix together the apples, brown sugar, 1 teaspoon of cinnamon and corn starch.

2. Arrange 1 egg roll wrapper onto a smooth surface.

3. Spread about 1 tablespoon of cream cheese over roll, leaving 1-inch of edges.

4. Place 1/3 cup of apple mixture over one corner of a wrapper, just below the center.

5. Fold the bottom corner over filling.

6. With wet fingers, moisten the remaining wrapper edges. Fold side corners toward center over filling.

7. Roll egg roll up tightly and with your fingers, press at tip to seal. Repeat with the remaining wrappers, cream cheese and filling. Arrange the rolls onto a cooking tray and spray with the cooking spray.

8. Arrange the drip pan in the bottom of Instant Vortex Plus Air Fryer Oven cooking chamber.

9. Select "Air Fry" and then adjust the temperature to 400 degrees F.

10. Set the timer for 12 minutes and press the "Start".

11. When the display shows "Add Food" insert the cooking tray in the center position.

12. When the display shows "Turn Food" turn the rolls and spray with the cooking spray.

13. Meanwhile, in a shallow dish, mix together the sugar and remaining cinnamon.

14. When cooking time is complete, remove the tray from Vortex.

15. Coat the hot egg rolls with sugar mixture and serve.

NUTRITION: Calories 236 Total Fat 5.7 g Saturated Fat 3.3 g Cholesterol 19 mg Sodium 229 mg Total Carbs 43.3 g Fiber 3 g Sugar 20.5 g Protein 4.5 g

20. __Cinnamon Donuts__

Basic Recipe

Preparation Time: 15 minutes

Cooking Time: 6 minutes

Servings: 8

INGREDIENTS:

- ½ cup granulated sugar

- 1 tablespoon ground cinnamon

- 1 (16.3-ounce) can flaky large biscuits

- Olive oil cooking spray

- 4 tablespoons unsalted butter, melted

DIRECTIONS:

1. Line a baking sheet with parchment paper. In a shallow dish, mix together the sugar and cinnamon. Set aside.

2. Remove the biscuits from the can and carefully, separate them. Place the biscuits onto the prepared baking sheet and with a 1-inch round biscuit cutter, cut holes from the center of each biscuit.

3. Place 4 donuts onto the lightly greased cooking pan in a single layer.

4. Arrange the drip pan in the bottom of Instant Vortex Plus Air Fryer Oven cooking chamber.

5. Select "Air Fry" and then adjust the temperature to 350 degrees F.

6. Set the timer for 6 minutes and press the "Start".

7. When the display shows "Add Food" insert the cooking tray in the center position.

8. When the display shows "Turn Food" turn the donuts.

9. When cooking time is complete, remove the tray from Vortex.

10. Brush both sides of the warm donuts with melted butter and then, coat with cinnamon sugar.

11. Repeat with the remaining donuts.

12. Serve warm.

NUTRITION: Calories 289   Total Fat 14.3 g Saturated Fat 5.5 g   Cholesterol 15 mg Sodium 590 mg Total Carbs 36.9 g Fiber 1.4 g Sugar 15.4 g Protein 3.9 g

CHAPTER 3:

Lunch

21.   Almond Flour Battered Wings

Basic Recipe

Preparation Time: 10 minutes

Cooking Time:25 minutes

Servings:4

INGREDIENTS:

- ¼ cup butter, melted

- ¾ cup almond flour

- 16 pieces chicken wings

- 2 tablespoons stevia powder

- 4 tablespoons minced garlic

- Salt and pepper to taste

DIRECTIONS:

1. Preheat the air fryer for 5 minutes. In a mixing bowl, combine the chicken wings, almond flour, stevia powder, and garlic Season with salt and pepper to taste.

2. Place in the air fryer basket and cook for 25 minutes at 4000F. Halfway through the cooking time, make sure that you give the fryer basket a shake. Once cooked, place in a bowl and drizzle with melted butter. Toss to coat.

NUTRITION: Calories 365 Carbs 7.8g Protein 23.7g Fat 26.9g

22.   <u>Baby Corn in Chili-Turmeric Spice</u>

Intermediate Recipe

Preparation Time: 5 minutes

Cooking Time: 8 minutes

Servings: 5

INGREDIENTS:

- ¼ cup water

- ¼ teaspoon baking soda

- ¼ teaspoon salt

- ¼ teaspoon turmeric powder

- ½ teaspoon curry powder

- ½ teaspoon red chili powder

- 1 cup chickpea flour or besan

- 10 pieces baby corn, Blanche

DIRECTIONS:

1. Preheat the air fryer to 4000F. Line the air fryer basket with aluminum foil and brush with oil.

2. In a mixing bowl, mix all ingredients except for the corn. Whisk until well combined.

3. Dip the corn in the batter and place inside the air fryer. Cook for 8 minutes until golden brown.

NUTRITION: Calories 89 Carbs 14.35g Protein 4.75g Fat 1.54g

23.   Baked Cheesy Eggplant with Marinara

Basic Recipe

Preparation Time: 15 minutes

Cooking Time: 45 minutes

Servings: 3

INGREDIENTS:

- 1 clove garlic, sliced

- 1 large eggplants

- 1 tablespoon olive oil

- 1 tablespoon olive oil

- 1/2 pinch salt, or as needed

- 1/4 cup and 2 tablespoons dry bread crumbs

- 1/4 cup and 2 tablespoons ricotta cheese

- 1/4 cup grated Parmesan cheese

- 1/4 cup grated Parmesan cheese

- 1/4 cup water, plus more as needed

- 1/4 teaspoon red pepper flakes

- 1-1/2 cups prepared marinara sauce

- 1-1/2 teaspoons olive oil

- 2 tablespoons shredded pepper jack cheese

- Salt and freshly ground black pepper to taste

DIRECTIONS:

1. Cut eggplant crosswise in 5 pieces. Peel and chop two pieces into ½-inch cubes.

2. Lightly grease baking pan of air fryer with 1 tablespoon olive oil. For 5 minutes, heat oil at 390oF. Add half eggplant strips and cook for 2 minutes per side. Transfer to a plate.

3. Add 1 ½ teaspoon olive oil and add garlic. Cook for a minute. Add chopped eggplants. Season with pepper flakes and salt. Cook for 4 minutes. Lower heat to 330oF and continue cooking eggplants until soft, around 8 minutes more.

4. Stir in water and marinara sauce. Cook for 7 minutes until heated through. Stirring every now and then. Transfer to a bowl.

5. In a bowl, whisk well pepper, salt, pepper jack cheese, Parmesan cheese, and ricotta. Evenly spread cheeses over eggplant strips and then fold in half.

6. Lay folded eggplant in baking pan. Pour marinara sauce on top.

7. In a small bowl whisk well olive oil, and bread crumbs. Sprinkle all over sauce.

8. Cook for 15 minutes at 390oF until tops are lightly browned.

9. Serve and enjoy.

NUTRITION: Calories 405 Carbs 41.1g Protein 12.7g Fat 21.4g

24.   <u>Baked Polenta with Chili-Cheese</u>

Basic Recipe

Preparation Time: 5 minutes

Cooking Time: 10 minutes

Servings: 3

INGREDIENTS:

- 1 commercial polenta roll, sliced

- 1 cup cheddar cheese sauce

- 1 tablespoon chili powder

DIRECTIONS:

1. Place the baking dish accessory in the air fryer.

2. Arrange the polenta slices in the baking dish.

3. Add the chili powder and cheddar cheese sauce.

4. Close the air fryer and cook for 10 minutes at 3900F.

NUTRITION: Calories 206 Carbs 25.3g Protein 3.2g Fat 4.2g

25.   Baked Portobello, Pasta 'n Cheese

Basic Recipe

Preparation Time: 10 minutes

Cooking Time: 30 minutes

Servings: 4

INGREDIENTS:

1. 1 cup milk

2. 1 cup shredded mozzarella cheese

3. 1 large clove garlic, minced

4. 1 tablespoon vegetable oil

5. 1/4 cup margarine

6. 1/4 teaspoon dried basil

7. 1/4-pound portobello mushrooms, thinly sliced

8. 2 tablespoons all-purpose flour

9. 2 tablespoons soy sauce

10. 4-ounce penne pasta, cooked according to manufacturer's Directions for Cooking

11. 5-ounce frozen chopped spinach, thawed

DIRECTIONS:

1. Lightly grease baking pan of air fryer with oil. For 2 minutes, heat on 360oF. Add mushrooms and cook for a minute. Transfer to a plate.

2. In same pan, melt margarine for a minute. Stir in basil, garlic, and flour. Cook for 3 minutes. Stir and cook for another 2 minutes. Stir in half of

milk slowly while whisking continuously. Cook for another 2 minutes. Mix well. Cook for another 2 minutes. Stir in remaining milk and cook for another 3 minutes.

3. Add cheese and mix well. Stir in soy sauce, spinach, mushrooms, and pasta. Mix well. Top with remaining cheese. Cook for 15 minutes at 390oF until tops are lightly browned. Serve and enjoy.

NUTRITION: Calories 482 Carbs 32.1g Protein 16.0g Fat 32.1g

26. Baked Potato Topped with Cream cheese 'n Olives

Basic Recipe Preparation Time: 10 minutes

Cooking Time:40 minutes

Servings:1

INGREDIENTS:

- ¼ teaspoon onion powder

- 1 medium russet potato, scrubbed and peeled

- 1 tablespoon chives, chopped

- 1 tablespoon Kalamata olives

- 1 teaspoon olive oil

- 1/8 teaspoon salt

- A dollop of vegan butter

- A dollop of vegan cream cheese

DIRECTIONS:

1. Place inside the air fryer basket and cook for 40 minutes. Be sure to turn the potatoes once halfway.

2. Place the potatoes in a mixing bowl and pour in olive oil, onion powder, salt, and vegan butter.

3. Preheat the air fryer to 4000F.

4. Serve the potatoes with vegan cream cheese, Kalamata olives, chives, and other vegan toppings that you want.

NUTRITION: Calories 504 Carbs 68.34g Protein 9.31g Fat 21.53g

27. Baked Zucchini Recipe from Mexico

Intermediate Recipe

Preparation Time: 10 minutes

Cooking Time: 30 minutes

Servings: 4

INGREDIENTS:

- 1 tablespoon olive oil
- 1-1/2 pounds zucchini, cubed
- 1/2 cup chopped onion
- 1/2 teaspoon garlic salt
- 1/2 teaspoon paprika
- 1/2 teaspoon dried oregano
- 1/2 teaspoon cayenne pepper, or to taste
- 1/2 cup cooked long-grain rice
- 1/2 cup cooked pinto beans
- 1-1/4 cups salsa
- 3/4 cup shredded Cheddar cheese

DIRECTIONS:

1. Lightly grease baking pan of air fryer with olive oil. Add onions and zucchini and for 10 minutes, cook on 360oF. Halfway through cooking time, stir.

2. Season with cayenne, oregano, paprika, and garlic salt. Mix well.

3. Stir in salsa, beans, and rice. Cook for 5 minutes.

4. Stir in cheddar cheese and mix well.

5. Cover pan with foil.

6. Cook for 15 minutes at 390oF until bubbly.

7. Serve and enjoy.

NUTRITION: Calories 263 Carbs 24.6g Protein 12.5g Fat 12.7g

28. <u>Banana Pepper Stuffed with Tofu 'n Spices</u>

Basic Recipe

Preparation Time: 5 minutes

Cooking Time: 10 minutes

Servings: 8

INGREDIENTS:

- ½ teaspoon red chili powder

- ½ teaspoon turmeric powder

- 1 onion, finely chopped

- 1 package firm tofu, crumbled

- 1 teaspoon coriander powder

- 3 tablespoons coconut oil

- 8 banana peppers, top end sliced and seeded

- Salt to taste

DIRECTIONS:

1. Preheat the air fryer for 5 minutes.

2. In a mixing bowl, combine the tofu, onion, coconut oil, turmeric powder, red chili powder, coriander power, and salt. Mix until well-combined.

3. Scoop the tofu mixture into the hollows of the banana peppers.

4. Place the stuffed peppers in the air fryer.

5. Close and cook for 10 minutes at 3250F.

NUTRITION: Calories 72 Carbs 4.1g Protein 1.2g Fat 5.6g

29.   Bell Pepper-Corn Wrapped in Tortilla

Intermediate Recipe

Preparation Time: 5 minutes

Cooking Time: 15 minutes

Servings: 4

INGREDIENTS:

- 1 small red bell pepper, chopped

- 1 small yellow onion, diced

- 1 tablespoon water

- 2 cobs grilled corn kernels

- 4 large tortillas

- 4 pieces commercial vegan nuggets, chopped

- Mixed greens for garnish

DIRECTIONS:

1. Preheat the air fryer to 4000F.

2. In a skillet heated over medium heat, water sauté the vegan nuggets together with the onions, bell peppers, and corn kernels. Set aside.

3. Place filling inside the corn tortillas.

4. Fold the tortillas and place inside the air fryer and cook for 15 minutes until the tortilla wraps are crispy.

5. Serve with mix greens on top.

NUTRITION: Calories 548 Carbs 43.54g Protein 46.73g Fat 20.76g

30. **<u>Black Bean Burger with Garlic-Chipotle</u>**

Intermediate Recipe

Preparation Time: 5 minutes

Cooking Time:20 minutes

Servings:3

INGREDIENTS:

- ½ cup corn kernels

- ½ teaspoon chipotle powder

- ½ teaspoon garlic powder

- ¾ cup salsa

- 1 ¼ teaspoon chili powder

- 1 ½ cup rolled oats

- 1 can black beans, rinsed and drained

- 1 tablespoon soy sauce

DIRECTIONS:

1. In a mixing bowl, combine all ingredients and mix using your hands.

2. Form small patties using your hands and set aside. Brush patties with oil if desired. Place the grill pan in the air fryer and place the patties on the grill pan accessory.

3. Close the lid and cook for 20 minutes on each side at 3300F. Halfway through the cooking time, flip the patties to brown the other side evenly

NUTRITION: Calories 395 Carbs 52.2g Protein 24.3g Fat 5.8g

31.   Spanish Brown Rice, Spinach 'n Tofu Frittata

Intermediate Recipe

Preparation Time: 15 minutes

Cooking Time: 55 minutes

Servings: 4

INGREDIENTS:

- ½ cup baby spinach, chopped

- ½ cup kale, chopped

- ½ onion, chopped

- ½ teaspoon turmeric

- 1 ¾ cups brown rice, cooked

- 1 flax egg (1 tablespoon flaxseed meal + 3 tablespoon cold water)

- 1 package firm tofu

- 1 tablespoon olive oil

- 1 yellow pepper, chopped

- 2 tablespoons soy sauce

- 2 teaspoons arrowroot powder

- 2 teaspoons Dijon mustard

- 2/3 cup almond milk

- 3 big mushrooms, chopped

- 3 tablespoons nutritional yeast

- 4 cloves garlic, crushed

- 4 spring onions, chopped

- A handful of basil leaves, chopped

DIRECTIONS:

1. Preheat the air fryer to 3750F. Grease a pan that will fit inside the air fryer. Prepare the frittata crust by mixing the brown rice and flax egg. Press the rice onto the baking dish until you form a crust. Brush with a little oil and cook for 10 minutes. Meanwhile, heat olive oil in a skillet over medium flame and sauté the garlic and onions for 2 minutes. Add the pepper and mushroom and continue stirring for 3 minutes.

2. Stir in the kale, spinach, spring onions, and basil. Remove from the pan and set aside. In a food processor, pulse together the tofu, mustard, turmeric, soy sauce, nutritional yeast, vegan milk and arrowroot powder. Pour in a mixing bowl and stir in the sautéed vegetables. Pour the vegan frittata mixture over the rice crust and cook in the air fryer for 40 minutes.

NUTRITION: Calories 226 Carbs 30.44g Protein 10.69g Fat 8.05g

32.   Brussels Sprouts with Balsamic Oil

Intermediate Recipe

Preparation Time: 5 minutes

Cooking Time: 15 minutes

Servings: 4

INGREDIENTS:

- ¼ teaspoon salt

- 1 tablespoon balsamic vinegar

- 2 cups Brussels sprouts, halved

- 2 tablespoons olive oil

DIRECTIONS:

1. Preheat the air fryer for 5 minutes.

2. Mix all ingredients in a bowl until the zucchini fries are well coated.

3. Place in the air fryer basket.

4. Close and cook for 15 minutes for 3500F.

NUTRITION: Calories 82 Carbs 4.6g Protein 1.5g Fat 6.8g

33.   <u>Buttered Carrot-Zucchini with Mayo</u>

Basic Recipe

Preparation Time: 10 minutes

Cooking Time: 25 minutes

Servings: 4

INGREDIENTS:

- 1 tablespoon grated onion

- 2 tablespoons butter, melted

- 1/2-pound carrots, sliced

- 1-1/2 zucchinis, sliced

- 1/4 cup water

- 1/4 cup mayonnaise

- 1/4 teaspoon prepared horseradish

- 1/4 teaspoon salt

- 1/4 teaspoon ground black pepper

- 1/4 cup Italian bread crumbs

DIRECTIONS:

1. Lightly grease baking pan of air fryer with cooking spray. Add carrots. For 8 minutes, cook on 360oF. Add zucchini and continue cooking for another 5 minutes.

2. Meanwhile, in a bowl whisk well pepper, salt, horseradish, onion, mayonnaise, and water. Pour into pan of veggies. Toss well to coat. In a small bowl mix melted butter and bread crumbs. Sprinkle over veggies.

3. Cook for 10 minutes at 390 F until tops are lightly browned.

4. Serve and enjoy.

NUTRITION: Calories 223 Carbs 13.8g Protein 2.7g Fat 17.4g

34.   Cauliflower Steak with Thick Sauce

Basic Recipe

Preparation Time: 5 minutes

Cooking Time: 15 minutes

Servings: 2

INGREDIENTS:

- ¼ cup almond milk

- ¼ teaspoon vegetable stock powder

- 1 cauliflower, sliced into two

- 1 tablespoon olive oil

- 2 tablespoons onion, chopped

- Salt and pepper to taste

DIRECTIONS:

1. Soak the cauliflower in salted water or brine for at least 2 hours. Preheat the air fryer to 4000F.

2. Rinse the cauliflower and place inside the air fryer and cook for 15 minutes. Meanwhile, heat oil in a skillet over medium flame. Sauté the onions and stir until translucent. Add the vegetable stock powder and milk.

3. Bring to boil and adjust the heat to low.

4. Allow the sauce to reduce and season with salt and pepper. Place cauliflower steak on a plate and pour over sauce.

NUTRITION: Calories 91 Carbs 6.58 g Protein 1.02g Fat 7.22g

35.   Cheddar, Squash 'n Zucchini Casserole

Intermediate Recipe

Preparation Time: 10 minutes

Cooking Time:30 minutes

Servings:4

INGREDIENTS:

- 1 egg

- 5 saltine crackers, or as needed, crushed

- 2 tablespoons bread crumbs

- 1/2-pound yellow squash, sliced

- 1/2-pound zucchini, sliced

- 1/2 cup shredded Cheddar cheese

- 1-1/2 teaspoons white sugar

- 1/2 teaspoon salt

- 1/4 onion, diced

- 1/4 cup biscuit baking mix

- 1/4 cup butter

DIRECTIONS:

1. Lightly grease baking pan of air fryer with cooking spray. Add onion, zucchini, and yellow squash. Cover pan with foil and for 15 minutes, cook on 360oF or until tender. Stir in salt, sugar, egg, butter, baking mix, and cheddar cheese. Mix well. Fold in crushed crackers. Top with bread

crumbs. Cook for 15 minutes at 390oF until tops are lightly browned. Serve and enjoy.

NUTRITION: Calories 285 Carbs 16.4g Protein 8.6g Fat 20.5g

CHAPTER 4:

Dinner

36. Pesto Tomatoes

Intermediate Recipe

Preparation Time: 5 minutes

Cooking Time: 14 minutes

Servings: 4

INGREDIENTS:

- Large heirloom tomatoes – 3, cut into ½ inch thick slices.

- 1 cup pesto

- 8 oz feta cheese, cut into ½ inch thick slices

- ½ cup red onion, sliced thinly

- 1 tablespoon olive oil

DIRECTIONS:

1. Spread some pesto on each slice of tomato. Top each tomato slice with a feta slice and onion and drizzle with oil. Arrange the tomatoes onto the greased rack and spray with cooking spray. Arrange the drip pan in the bottom of the Instant Vortex Air Fryer Oven cooking chamber. Select "Air Fry" and then adjust the temperature to 390 °F. Set the time for 14 minutes and press "Start". When the display shows "Add Food" insert the rack in

the center position. When the display shows "Turn Food" do not turn food. When cooking time is complete, remove the rack from the Vortex Oven.Serve warm.

NUTRITION: Calories 480 Carbs 13g Fat 41.9g Protein 15.4g

37.   <u>Herbed Potatoes</u>

Basic Recipe

Preparation Time: 5 minutes

Cooking Time:20 minutes

Servings:4

INGREDIENTS:

- 1 lb small red potatoes, cut into 1-inch pieces

- 1 tablespoon olive oil

- 1 teaspoon chopped fresh thyme

- 1 teaspoon chopped fresh rosemary

- 1 teaspoon chopped fresh oregano

- salt and ground black pepper, as required

- 1 tablespoon grate lemon zest

DIRECTIONS:

1. In a bowl, add all ingredients except lemon zest and toss to coat well. Place the potatoes in the rotisserie basket and attach the lid. Arrange the drip pan in the bottom of the Instant Vortex Air Fryer Oven cooking chamber. Select "Air Fry" and then adjust the temperature to 400 °F. Set the time for 20 minutes and press "Start". Then, close the door and touch "Rotate". When the display shows "Add Food" arrange the rotisserie basket, on the rotisserie spit. Then, close the door and touch "Rotate". When cooking time is complete, press the red lever to release the rod. Remove from the

Vortex and transfer the potatoes into a bowl. Add the lemon zest and toss to coat well. Serve immediately.

NUTRITION: Calories 112 Carbs 18.7g Fat 3.7g Protein 2.2g

38.   **Seasoned Potatoes**

Basic Recipe

Preparation Time: 10 minutes

Cooking Time: 40 minutes

Servings: 1

INGREDIENTS:

- 2 russet potatoes, scrubbed

- ½ tablespoon butter, melted

- ½ teaspoon garlic & herb blend seasoning

- ½ teaspoon garlic powder

- Salt, as required

DIRECTIONS:

1. In a small bowl, mix together spices and salt. With a fork, prick the potatoes. Coat the potatoes with butter and sprinkle with spice mixture. Arrange the potatoes onto the cooking rack. Arrange the drip pan in the bottom of the Instant Vortex Air Fryer Oven cooking chamber. Select "Air Fry" and then adjust the temperature to 400 °F. Set the time for 40 minutes and press "Start". When the display shows "Add Food" insert the cooking rack in the center position. When the display shows "Turn Food" do nothing. When cooking time is complete, remove the tray from the Vortex Oven. Serve hot.

NUTRITION: Calories 176 Carbs 34.2g Fat 2.1g Protein 3.8g

39. <u>Cheesy Spinach</u>

Basic Recipe Preparation Time: 5 minutes

Cooking Time: 15 minutes

Servings: 3

INGREDIENTS:

- Frozen spinach – 1 (10-oz.) Package, thawed

- ½ cup onion, chopped

- 2 teaspoon minced garlic

- 4 oz cream cheese. Chopped

- ½ teaspoon ground nutmeg

- Salt and ground black pepper, as required

- ¼ cup parmesan cheese, shredded

DIRECTIONS:

1. In a bowl, mix together spinach, onion, garlic, cream cheese, nutmeg, salt, and black pepper.Place the spinach mixture into a baking dish that will fit in the Vortex Air Fryer Oven. Arrange the drip pan in the bottom of the Instant Vortex Air Fryer Oven cooking chamber. Select "Air Fry" and then adjust the temperature to 355 °F. Set the time for 15 minutes and press "Start". When the display shows "Add Food" insert the baking dish in the center position. When the display shows "Turn Food" do not turn food. When cooking time is complete, remove the baking dish from the Vortex Oven. Serve hot.

NUTRITION: Calories 194 Carbs 7.3g Fat 15.5g Protein 8.4g

40.   Spicy Zucchini

Basic Recipe

Preparation Time: 10 minutes

Cooking Time: 12 minutes

Servings: 3

INGREDIENTS:

- Zucchini – 1 lb. Cut into ½-inch thick slices lengthwise

- 1 tablespoon olive oil

- ½ teaspoon garlic powder

- ½ teaspoon cayenne pepper

- Salt and ground black pepper, as required

DIRECTIONS:

1. Add all the ingredients into a bowl and toss to coat well. Arrange the zucchini slices onto a cooking tray.

2. Arrange the drip pan in the bottom of the Instant Vortex Air Fryer Oven cooking chamber. Select "Air Fry" and then adjust the temperature to 400 °F. Set the time for 12 minutes and press "Start".

3. When the display shows "Add Food" insert the cooking tray in the center position. When the display shows "Turn Food" do nothing. When cooking time is complete, remove the tray from the Vortex Oven. Serve hot.

NUTRITION: Calories 67 Carbs 5.6g Fat 5g Protein 2g

41. <u>Seasoned Yellow Squash</u>

Basic Recipe

Preparation Time: 5 minutes

Cooking Time:6 minutes

Servings:2

INGREDIENTS:

- 4 large yellow squash, cut into slices

- ¼ cup olive oil

- ½ onion, sliced

- ¾ teaspoon italian seasoning

- ½ teaspoon garlic salt

- ¼ teaspoon seasoned salt

DIRECTIONS:

1. In a large bowl, mix together all the ingredients. Place the veggie mixture in the greased cooking tray.

2. Arrange the drip pan in the bottom of Instant Vortex Air Fryer Oven cooking chamber. Select "Air Fry" and then adjust the temperature to 400 °F.

3. Set the time for 10 minutes and press "Start". When the display shows "Add Food" insert the cooking tray in the center position.

4. When the display shows "Turn Food" turn the vegetables. When cooking time is complete, remove the tray from the Vortex Oven. Serve hot.

NUTRITION: Calories 113 Carbs 8.1g Fat 9g Protein 4.2g

42.   <u>Buttered Asparagus</u>

Basic Recipe

Preparation Time: 5 minutes

Cooking Time:10 minutes

Servings:3

INGREDIENTS:

- 1 lb. trimmed Fresh thick asparagus spears

- 1 tablespoon melted Butter

- Salt and ground black pepper, as required

DIRECTIONS:

1. Add all the ingredients into a bowl and toss to coat well. Arrange the asparagus onto a cooking tray. Arrange the drip pan in the bottom of Instant Vortex Air Fryer Oven cooking chamber. Select "Air Fry" and then adjust the temperature to 350 °F. Set the time for 10 minutes and press "Start". When the display shows "Add Food" insert the cooking tray in the center position. When the display shows "Turn Food" turn the asparagus. When cooking time is complete, remove the tray from Vortex Oven. Serve hot.

NUTRITION: Calories 64 Carbs 5.9g Fat 4g Protein 3.4g

43.   **Balsamic Brussels Sprouts**

Basic Recipe

Preparation Time: 10 minutes

Cooking Time: 20 minutes

Servings: 4

INGREDIENTS:

- Brussels sprouts – 1 lb. Ends trimmed and cut into bite-sized pieces

- 1 tablespoon balsamic vinegar

- 1 tablespoon olive oil

- Salt and ground black pepper, as required

DIRECTIONS:

1. Add all the ingredients into a bowl and toss to coat well. Place the Brussels Sprouts in the rotisserie basket and attach the lid. Arrange the drip pan in the bottom of Instant Vortex Air Fryer Oven cooking chamber. Select "Air Fry" and then adjust the temperature to 350 °F. Set the time for 20 minutes and press "Start". Then, close the door and touch "Rotate". When the display shows "Add Food" arrange the rotisserie basket, on the rotisserie spit. Then, close the door and touch "Rotate". When cooking time is complete, press the red lever to release the rod. Remove from the Vortex Oven. Serve hot.

NUTRITION: Calories 80 Carbs 10.3g Fat 3.9g Protein 3.9g

44.   Parmesan Broccoli

Basic Recipe

Preparation Time: 5 minutes

Cooking Time:6 minutes

Servings:4

INGREDIENTS:

- 1 lb. small broccoli florets

- 1 tablespoon minced garlic

- 2 tbsps. olive oil

- ¼ cup parmesan cheese, grated

DIRECTIONS:

1. Add all the ingredients into a bowl and toss to coat well. Arrange the broccoli florets onto a cooking tray.

2. Arrange the drip pan in the bottom of the Instant Vortex Air Fryer Oven cooking chamber. Select "Air Fry" and then adjust the temperature to 350 °F.

3. Set the time for 6 minutes and press "Start". When the display shows "Add Food" insert the cooking tray in the center position.

4. When the display shows "Turn Food" turn the broccoli florets. When cooking time is complete, remove the tray from Vortex Oven. Serve hot.

NUTRITION: Calories 112 Carbs 18.7g Fat 3.7g Protein 2.2g

45. **Buttered Broccoli**

Basic Recipe

Preparation Time: 5 minutes

Cooking Time: 15 minutes

Servings: 4

INGREDIENTS:

- 1 lb. broccoli florets

- 1 tablespoon melted butter

- ½ teaspoon crushed red pepper flakes

- Salt and ground black pepper, as required

DIRECTIONS:

1. Add all the ingredients into a bowl and toss to coat well. Place the broccoli florets in the rotisserie basket and attach the lid. Arrange the drip pan in the bottom of the Instant Vortex Air Fryer Oven cooking chamber. Select "Air Fry" and then adjust the temperature to 400 °F. Set the time for 15 minutes and press "Start".

2. Then, close the door and touch "Rotate". When the display shows "Add Food" arrange the rotisserie basket, on the rotisserie spit. Then, close the door and touch "Rotate". When cooking time is complete, press the red lever to release the rod. Remove from the Vortex Oven. Serve immediately.

NUTRITION: Calories 55 Carbs 6.1g Fat 3g Protein 2.3g

46. Greek Buffalo Cauliflower

Basic Recipe

Preparation Time: 10 minutes

Cooking Time:12 minutes

Servings:4

INGREDIENTS:

- 1 large head cauliflower, cut into bite-size florets

- 1 tablespoon olive oil

- 2 teaspoon garlic powder

- Salt and ground black pepper, as required

- 1 tablespoon melted butter

- 2/3 cup warm buffalo sauce

DIRECTIONS:

1. In a large bowl, add cauliflower florets, oil, garlic powder, salt and black pepper and toss to coat. Arrange the cauliflower florets onto the greased cooking tray in a single layer. Arrange the drip pan in the bottom of the Instant Vortex Air Fryer Oven cooking chamber. Select "Air Fry" and then adjust the temperature to 375 °F. Set the time for 12 minutes and press "Start". When the display shows "Add Food" insert the cooking tray in the center position. When the display shows "Turn Food" coat the cauliflower florets with buffalo sauce.

2. When cooking time is complete, remove the tray from Vortex Oven. Serve hot.

NUTRITION: Calories 102 Carbs 5.2g Fat 9g Protein 1.7g

47. Cauliflower with Tofu

Basic Recipe Preparation Time: 5 minutes

Cooking Time: 15 minutes

Servings: 2

INGREDIENTS:

- 7-oz firm tofu. pressed and cubed
- ½small head cauliflower, cut into florets
- 1 tablespoon canola oil
- 1 tablespoon nutritional yeast
- ¼ teaspoon dried parsley
- 1 teaspoon ground turmeric
- ¼ teaspoon paprika
- Salt and ground black pepper, as required

DIRECTIONS:

1. In a bowl, mix together the tofu, cauliflower and the remaining ingredients. Place the tofu mixture in the greased cooking tray. Arrange the drip pan in the bottom of the Instant Vortex Air Fryer Oven cooking chamber. Select "Air Fry" and then adjust the temperature to 390 °F. Set the time for 15 minutes and press "Start". When the display shows "Add Food" insert the cooking tray in the center position.

2. When the display shows "Turn Food" turn the tofu mixture. When cooking time is complete, remove the tray from the Vortex Oven. Serve hot.

NUTRITION: Calories 170 Carbs 8.3g Fat 11.6g Protein 11.9g

48. Carrots with Green Beans

Basic Recipe

Preparation Time: 5 minutes

Cooking Time: 10 minutes

Servings: 3

INGREDIENTS:

- ½ lb green beans. trimmed

- ½ lb carrots, peeled and cut into sticks

- 1 tablespoon olive oil

- Salt and ground black pepper, as required

DIRECTIONS:

1. Add all the ingredients into a bowl and toss to coat well. Place the vegetables in the rotisserie basket and attach the lid. Arrange the drip pan in the bottom of the Instant Vortex Air Fryer Oven cooking chamber. Select "Air Fry" and then adjust the temperature to 400 °F. Set the time for 10 minutes and press "Start". Then, close the door and touch "Rotate". When the display shows "Add Food" arrange the rotisserie basket, on the rotisserie spit. Then, close the door and touch "Rotate". When cooking time is complete, press the red lever to release the rod. Remove from the Vortex Oven. Serve hot.

NUTRITION: Calories 94, Carbs 12.7g Fat 4.8g Protein 2g

49.   **Bell Peppers with Potatoes**

Basic Recipe

Preparation Time: 5 minutes

Cooking Time:6 minutes

Servings:2

INGREDIENTS:

- 2 cups Water

- russet potatoes 5, peeled and cubed

- ½ tablespoon extra-virgin olive oil –

- ½onion, chopped

- ½jalapeño pepper, chopped

- 1large bell pepper, seeded and chopped

- ¼ teaspoon crushed dried oregano

- ¼ teaspoon garlic powder

- ¼ teaspoon ground cumin

- ¼ teaspoon red chili powder

- Salt and ground black pepper, as required

DIRECTIONS:

1. In a large bowl, add the water and potatoes and set aside for about 30 minutes. Drain well and pat dry with the paper towels. In a bowl, add the potatoes and oil and toss to coat well. Arrange the potato cubes onto the greased rack. Arrange the drip pan in the bottom of Instant Vortex Air Fryer Oven cooking chamber. Select "Air Fry" and then adjust the

temperature to 330 °F. Set the time for 5 minutes and press "Start". When the display shows "Add Food" insert the cooking rack in the center position. When the display shows "Turn Food" do not turn food. When cooking time is complete, remove the tray from the Vortex Oven. Transfer the potato cubes into a large bowl with remaining ingredients and toss to coat well. Place the veggie mixture onto the greased cooking pan and spread in an even layer. Select "Air Fry" and then adjust the temperature to 390 °F. Set the time for 20 minutes and press "Start". When the display shows "Add Food" insert the cooking rack in the center position. When the display shows "Turn Food" turn the vegetables. When cooking time is complete, remove the tray from the Vortex Oven. Serve hot.

NUTRITION: Calories 216 Carbs 45.7g Fat 2.2g Protein 5g

50. Mushrooms with Peas

Basic Recipe

Preparation Time: 10 minutes

Cooking Time: 16 minutes

Servings: 4

INGREDIENTS:

- ½ cup soy sauce

- 4 tbsps maple syrup

- 4 tbsps rice vinegar

- 4 Garlic cloves, chopped finely

- 2 teaspoon Chinese five-spice powder

- ½ teaspoon Ground ginger

- 16 oz.Cremini mushrooms, halved

- ½ cup Frozen peas

DIRECTIONS:

1. Grease a baking dish that will fit in the Vortex Air Fryer Oven. In a bowl, add the soy sauce, maple syrup, vinegar, garlic, five-spice powder, and ground ginger and mix well. Set aside. Place the mushroom into the prepared baking dish in a single layer. Arrange the drip pan in the bottom of the Instant Vortex Air Fryer Oven cooking chamber. Select "Air Fry" and then adjust the temperature to 350 °F. Set the time for 15 minutes and press "Start". When the display shows "Add Food" insert the baking dish in the center position. When the display shows "Turn Food" add the peas

and vinegar mixture into the baking dish and stir to combine. When cooking time is complete, remove the baking dish from the Vortex Oven. Serve hot.

NUTRITION: Calories 132 Carbs 25g Fat 0.3g Protein 6.1g

Conclusion

This is it! You have worked your way through this book. We hope that some of your misgivings about starting out with your brand-new kitchen helper have been put to rest. Remember, every person starts out being a beginner; we all have to learn what works best for us personally. Each time you make a new dish, you learn more and your experience grows.

Air fryers recreate the customary browning of foods by coursing hot air around food as opposed to submerging the food in oil. Similarly, as with searing, appropriately arranged foods are fresh, succulent, brilliant dark-colored, and delightful.

An air-fryer cooker or appliances is a convection oven in smaller than expected – a conservative round and hollow ledge convection oven, to be accurate (have a go at saying that multiple times quick).

We all are fan of good food. It's not just our fuel, it's our mood manipulator. We all know how important it is to eat healthy when we are so hungry that we forget what healthy is. We often eat what we find most accessible. So why not make the good things most easy to have. I know things not always go as we expect. You will always find other attractions. But from now i believe you can trust on this book to overcome those others as you know you can make that same thing healthier with the least possible time. I definitely am not bragging about it. Many chiefs have confirmed that an air fryer can make it healthier and quicker. This is even not an alternative of oven; it is unique by its own in the sense of through Cooking. There are a lot of recipes that we have now, and i guess it will help us experiment a bit deeper with our taste. It is also something to trust on while on vacation. As it always cooks the food thoroughly; so, you can depend on this when you are relaxing in a recreational vehicle with your favorite music on. For all these and a lot of unspoken reasons my confidence is on the air fryer and the taste that the recipes will serve. I will be very happy to know your honest opinions. Insights are always the motivation for next work. Please let me know what you think. Live healthy, live strong.

This is truly the healthiest way to prepare food that everyone in the family will enjoy and keep coming back for more without them even realizing that they are eating better.

Now you know everything you need to in order to get started with your air fryer! Just pick a recipe to get started with low Sodium, low carb Cooking in no time at all. Remember that healthy food doesn't mean that you need to slave away in the kitchen or pay big bucks for hand delivered meals. All you need is to try new, delicious recipes that are sure to become family favorites in no time at all. Your air fryer will soon be the most used item in your kitchen!

CPSIA information can be obtained
at www.ICGtesting.com
Printed in the USA
LVHW020515150221
679326LV00004B/606

9 781801 683524